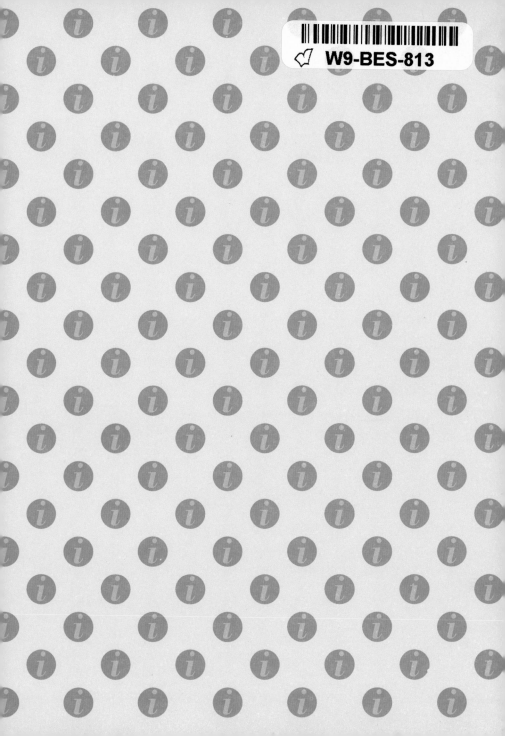

IDENTIFYING

DINOSAURS

The new compact study guide and identifier

DINOSAURS

The new compact study guide and identifier

Steve Parker

CHARTWELL
BOOKS, INC.

A QUINTET BOOK

Published by Chartwell Books
A Division of Book Sales, Inc.
114, Northfield Avenue
Edison, New Jersey 08837

ISBN 0-7858-0775-6

This book was designed and produced by
Quintet Publishing Limited
6 Blundell Street
London N7 9BH

Creative Director: Richard Dewing
Art Director: Anne Brady
Designer: Michael Head
Project Editor: Clare Hubbard
Editor: Emma Callery

Typeset in Great Britain by
Central Southern Typesetters, Eastbourne
Manufactured in Singapore by Bright Arts Pte. Ltd.
Printed in China by Leefung-Asco Printers Ltd.

All illustrations by Elizabeth Sawyer except: Danny
McBride pages 7, 12; Graham Rosewarne pages 5, 33 t,
42, 62, 67, 69, 72; Jim Robins page 20.

Symbols designed by Nigel Coath at ProCreative.

The material in this publication
previously appeared in *Dinosaur
Identifier* by Steve Parker

CONTENTS

ORIGINS OF THE DINOSAURS

At the beginning of the Mesozoic era, 245 million years ago, the world map was very different from today. All the main land masses were joined together into one enormous lump, the supercontinent of Pangaea. Since that time the continents have gradually moved apart and taken up their present positions. We know that dinosaurs populated just about all of Pangaea, and every continent resulting from its breakup, since their fossils have been found worldwide.

During the Triassic (the first period of the Mesozoic era), sea levels were low and more dry land was exposed compared to today. A greater proportion of sedimentary rocks, which are usually formed beneath the sea, were laid down on land at this time. The types of sandstones produced during these long-gone millenia indicate an arid, desert-like climate. Nowadays the centers of the large continents, especially Africa, Asia, and Australia, are dry, desert regions; so it is likely that the huge area of Pangaea had vast regions subjected to an arid climate. The animals and plants must have been well adapted to hot, dry conditions.

MASS EXTINCTION

The end of the Permian period, the last geological period of the Palaeozoic era, was marked by an enormous decrease in the diversity of fossils in the rocks. Our conclusion is that there was a mass extinction – indeed, the greatest mass extinction found throughout the fossil record. Many animals disappeared quite suddenly, in geological terms. The dinosaurs themselves and many other animals were to suffer the same fate, 160 million years later.

Fossils tell us that mass extinctions have punctuated the history of life at many intervals. The reasons for their occurrence are largely unknown, but a reasonable guess is that they reflect some drastic change which many animals could not survive at the time or evolve fast enough to counteract.

The drifting of the continents during prehistory. At the beginning of the Triassic period the continents were joined together in one huge supercontinent, called Pangaea. As the Jurassic period took over, a rift appeared which became the Atlantic Ocean, as North America moved westwards. The supercontinent of Gondwanaland, consisting of South America, Africa, India, Antarctica, and Australia, began to move away from Europe in the Jurassic. During the Cretaceous period, Gondwanaland split gradually into the continents we know today. The distribution of similar dinosaur fossils on different continents is explained by this process.

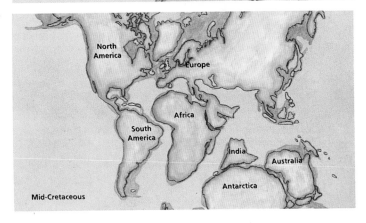

In the seas after the catastrophic "end-of-Permian event" the ammonites flourished rapidly, although they had survived through only one group of their kind. Shellfish such as brachiopods and mollusc bivalves also survived, but many of the other invertebrate groups were severely depleted. From this disaster was born the Age of Reptiles. Although there were many sharks and other fish in the seas, the dominant predators came to be huge marine reptiles such as ichthyosaurs ("fish-lizards") and nothosaurs.

A FLOWERLESS LANDSCAPE

On land, the predominant plants of the time were the gymnosperms, plants that had no covering to their seeds. They included the cycads, gingkos, and conifers. They were tough and woody, they did not have flowers; and they bore their seeds on types of cone. Ecologically, they provided food and shelter for millipedes, centipedes, scorpions, spiders, and insects.

Previously the amphibians had feasted on these hordes, but their continued dependence on water meant that they did not flourish in the new, arid climate. As the ponds, lakes, and rivers dried up, the amphibians died back. However, the conditions now suited the burgeoning reptiles very well. Some reptilian groups were already thriving as they diversified to take advantage of the opportunities offered. The Age of Amphibians was history. The reptiles were taking over.

EGGS WITH SHELLS

Reptiles were the first vertebrate animals to lay eggs surrounded by an amniotic membrane. The key to their former dominance on land, these membranes enclose a watery environment in which the embryo can develop regardless of the presence or absence of water outside. The egg also has a leathery, waterproof shell for added protection. Other reptile innovations were a waterproof skin, and more specialized teeth to cope with a variety of foods.

It is often thought that dinosaurs were the "first and best" of the prehistoric reptiles, and that other reptilian groups trailed along in their wake. Not so. There were many other types of reptile during the Permian and Triassic periods, before the dinosaurs rose to prominence. They included the herbivorous rhynchosaurs, and also the tremendously successful mammal-like reptiles. These creatures had the same skull openings as mammals and also more complicated teeth than other reptiles. They evolved into many forms as amphibians faded from the scene.

CONVERGENT EVOLUTION

We can use the theory of evolution to classify animals and interpret their evolutionary relationships. Animals evolving from one type to another retain many of their shared characteristics, inherited from their common ancestor. Thus the more shared characteristics the two animals have in common, the closer they are in evolutionary terms. However, nature can play tricks. The forces of evolution sometimes mean that two unrelated groups of animals faced with the same problem, come up with the same "design solution." This is called convergent evolution. It occurs throughout the fossil record and can make us draw false evolutionary relationships. One familiar example is the wing. This has evolved independently in many groups of animals. Living bats possess wings that look similar on the outside to those of extinct pterosaurs, yet inside, the bone arrangements are quite different. This shows that the wings must have evolved independently.

ABOVE *One of the most successful groups of reptiles in the Triassic, before the dinosaurs reached their peak, were the rhynchosaurs. They were abundant, though only for a relatively short time, and about the size of a large pig. They had a beak-like upper jaw and tusks in the lower jaw, which they probably used to grub about on the forest floor, searching for roots and shoots.*

Some were lumbering plant-eaters, others carved a living as nimble carnivores. Some, like the well-known *Dimetrodon*, had sail-shaped protrusions on their backs to help with temperature regulation. They were collectively the "ruling reptiles" of the Permian and early Triassic periods.

The ancestors of the dinosaurs and their kin had already appeared in the Permian period. These small diapsids were very successful and today their descendents, the lepidosaurs, are the predominant reptile group – as the lizards.

At some stage there was a split in

this line of evolution and larger reptiles appeared on a new branch of the evolutionary tree. These were the archosaurs or "ruling reptiles," a group which includes the dinosaurs, pterosaurs, and crocodiles. These were to flourish throughout the Jurassic and Cretaceous periods.

DINOSAUR BEGINNINGS

Archosaurs were first represented by thecodonts, who had serrated teeth fixed into sockets in their jaws, rather than embedded in the toughened skin of the mouth as in more primitive animals. They looked similar to crocodiles. They were heavily built, with powerful hindlimbs, and some had bony plates along their back – suggestive of the armor later found in some dinosaurs. Their legs had moved from the inefficient lizard-like, sprawling-sideways position, to a position partly beneath the body in a semi-upright posture. These animals continued to evolve during the Triassic period.

By the beginning of the Jurassic period, the early dinosaurs were established. They were lightweight, carnivorous animals. Their legs had moved to a position completely beneath the body, to give an erect limb posture, and they had adopted a bipedal (two-legged) method of locomotion.

Among the first dinosaurs were the theropods. *Coelophysis* was one of the earliest. It appeared about 225 million years ago. Footprints found in rocks on a Welsh shoreline are believed to have been made by this type of dinosaur. This agile creature had long jaws, and claws on its fingers. It would have chased and eaten amphibians, small reptiles, and possibly early mammals that shared its world. This original two-legged dinosaur design was so successful that it continued throughout their evolution.

IN THE SEAS AND SKIES

During the Jurassic period, from 208 million to 144 million years ago, the sea level rose and the two massive continents of Gondwanaland and Laurasia became separated by shallow seas. The climate was warmer than today, moist in some parts and arid in others. Conditions were ideal for life in all its forms.

A great variety of invertebrates lived in the seas, where ammonites still flourished. Reptiles had conquered land, sea, and air by this time. Plesiosaurs, ichthyosaurs, crocodiles, and turtles swam in the waters, while pterosaurs flew overhead. A new group of creatures was just beginning to appear. The first bird, *Archaeopteryx*, emerged about 160 million years ago. It had some reptilian characteristics and some

avian. It had a covering of feathers, and a wishbone to strengthen its chest for the stresses and strains of flapping flight, but it still had teeth in its mouth, like a reptile, and its spinal bones continued into a tail. Birds must have continued their evolution after this time, but their fragile, lightweight bones break easily and so their fossils are rare. It was not until after the Mesozoic era that they achieved a short period of dominance on land.

Forests of gymnosperm trees flourished and new land creatures appeared to harvest the insects and other small animals that lived there. The first mammals were the small, nocturnal, shrew-like creatures of more than 200 million years ago. They were covered with fur, and we assume that like mammals today, they could maintain their body temperature, so being able to remain active during cold weather. They had good eyesight and

ABOVE The crocodile group stems from the same origins as the dinosaurs. Protosuchus *was a crocodile that lived in the late Triassic period. It had a wide head with a narrow nose and long legs; it was probably more land-based than modern crocodiles.*

large brains. They also had amniotic membranes to protect their young, and these early mammals probably laid eggs. Eventually the embryo with its membranes was retained within the abdomen of the mother, until it was developed enough to survive outside. The young were then nourished with milk from the mammary glands (which give the group its name).

Mammals were therefore around during the whole of the Age of Dinosaurs, but in terms of numbers and variety they could not compete with their scaly contemporaries. They survived and evolved in the dinosaurs'

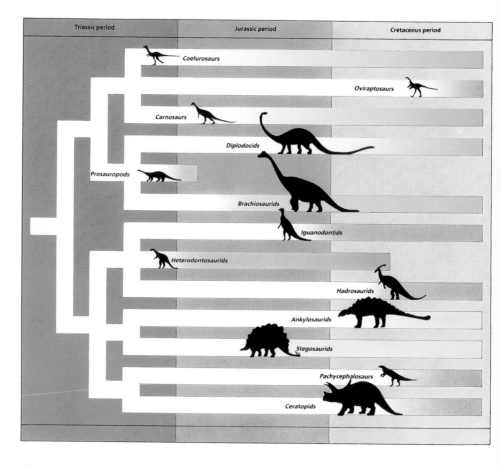

| Triassic period | Jurassic period | Cretaceous period |

Coelurosaurs

Oviraptosaurs

Carnosaurs

Diplodocids

Prosauropods

Brachiosaurids

Iguanodontids

Heterodontosaurids

Hadrosaurids

Ankylosaurids

Stegosaurids

Pachycephalosaurs

Ceratopids

This chart shows representatives of the main groups of dinosaurs and when they appeared. We know approximately when they lived, because we know the age of the rocks in which their fossils are found. Triassic rocks, from 245 to about 208 million years ago, contain the earliest dinosaurs. During the Jurassic period, until about 144 million years ago, the great diversification took place and more dinosaur groups appeared. The Cretaceous period, until 65 million years ago, showed continuing diversification before rapid decline.

shadow until the time was right, at the beginning of the Cenozoic era, for their rise to dominance.

During the Jurassic period, the dinosaurs came into their own. They evolved along two main lines: bipedal meat-eaters and quadrupedal plant-eaters. By the end of the Jurassic period, dinosaurs had taken over most terrestrial habitats and were the dominant land creatures.

DINOSAUR DOMINANCE

During the Cretaceous period there was extensive continental flooding. Thick layers of chalk, formed from the tiny shells of planktonic organisms, were laid down beneath these seas. The vast land masses had split into the continents we know today, and they had begun to drift slowly towards their present positions. The climate was mild across most of the world. There was still a great diversity of animals and plants in the sea and on land. Flowering plants appeared and slowly displaced the gymnosperms. Mammals continued to evolve into varied, but still generally small forms.

But it was the dinosaurs that ruled the land. All the famous creatures we know from childhood books lived at this time, including incredibly ferocious meat-eaters and some of the biggest animals ever to walk the Earth. There were huge dinosaurs with spectacular armor. Some, from the evidence of fossils, had complex social behavior.

Everything written about dinosaurs comes from educated guesswork based on fossil evidence combined with comparative anatomy. We will never know how near we are to the truth about these animals, but it seems that they lived similar lives and coped with similar ecological challenges to the animals of today. Finding food, escaping predation, and producing young were the driving forces in the past that influenced how they evolved, just as they are in the present.

Reptiles, as we have seen, had their origins among the amphibians. The reptile lines of evolution include the turtles, which have remained almost unchanged to the present day; the ichthyosaurs, which died out; the lizards and later the snakes, both of which flourish today; the mammal-like reptiles; and the thecodonts. The thecodont reptiles probably split into crocodiles, pterosaurs, birds, and the various groups of dinosaurs – the groups we call the archosaurs, or "ruling reptiles."

DINOSAUR GROUPS

EARLY DINOSAURS

SAURISCHIANS

Dinosaurs are not a neat group of animals at the end of one branch of evolution. There are many different types, and their evolutionary relationships are unclear. They may not even belong to a single overall group. However, it seems that the thecodonts split into two distinct lines or taxonomic orders: the Saurischian dinosaurs and the Ornithischian dinosaurs.

The classification of the two orders of dinosaurs is based on two different sorts of hip bone arrangement found in dinosaur skeletons. The Saurischian (or "lizard-hipped") bone structure is similar to that of other reptiles, with the pubic bone pointing down and forwards. The Ornithischian (or "bird-hipped") pubic bones point down and backwards, alongside the ischium bone, as it does in birds today. Strangely, it is thought that birds themselves probably did not evolve from this group but from the lizard-hipped stock; their hips became "bird-like" much later.

The Saurischian dinosaurs had both herbivorous and carnivorous representatives. The theropods, the meat-eating Saurischian dinosaurs, were mostly bipedal animals. Some were large and heavy with effective teeth, such as *Tyrannosaurus*. Others were small, slender, and fleet of foot, such as the coelurosaurs and ostrich dinosaurs. Some of these animals evolved to take advantage of the glut of herbivores, since there were few other predators to compete with them. Others depended for food mainly on insects, small reptiles, and similar creatures of the time; their main competition for such food came from the nocturnal mammals of the time.

The herbivorous Saurischians, the sauropods, included some of the largest land animals that ever lived,

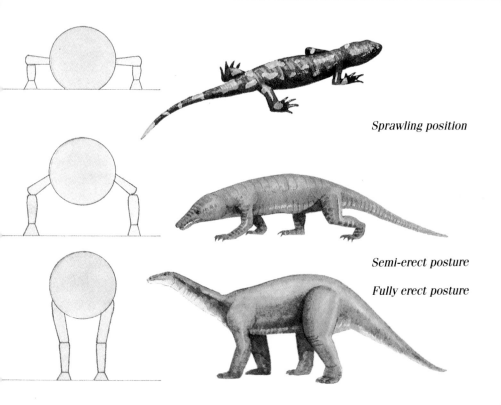

Sprawling position

Semi-erect posture

Fully erect posture

such as the familiar *Diplodocus* and *Brachiosaurus.* This group spans the whole dinosaur fossil record but most members retained the characteristic "diplodocid" features, with only minor variations. The design was obviously ideally suited for their way of life, as the shark is perfectly suited to the ocean. It was adaptable in changing conditions, and needed no excessive modification.

Both the Saurischian and Ornithischian orders of dinosaurs lost the sprawling gait of most reptiles,

ABOVE *The development of reptile posture. Lizards have a sprawling posture, their legs held out from the side of the body. Crocodilians, such as* Riojasuchus, *have adopted a semi erect posture with the body being held clear of the ground, but the limbs still somewhat sprawling. The dinosaurs had a fully erect posture, like mammals and birds.*

and instead they held their legs beneath their bodies. This carried the body weight more efficiently and so the dinosaurs were probably more agile than the less advanced quadrupeds such as amphibians. Otherwise the two orders of dinosaurs had little in common.

The Saurischians appeared first. To begin with they were all bipedal carnivores, and one group, the theropods, remained so until the dinosaurs' end. One of the earliest theropods was *Herrerasaurus*, whose fossils come from the Andes mountains in Argentina. It was the

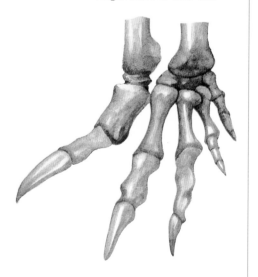

ABOVE Plateosaurus *was an early plant-eating dinosaur. The posture puzzled palaeontologists for some time, as the body did not seem to be balanced correctly for a bipedal animal, yet the arms and hands did not seem designed for walking. However, further studies of the finger joints suggest that the hands could be bent forwards for grasping vegetation, as well as backwards like toes for walking.*

size of a large dog but ran on its two larger back legs – a design followed for millions of years.

The other branch of Saurischians, however, returned to a quadrupedal, vegetarian way of life. Even in the early stages their size increased to reach proportions never seen on land before, and rarely since. An early representative was *Plateosaurus*, whose fossils are found in upper Triassic rocks. A smaller version of the early sauropods, or prosauropods, was *Anchisaurus*, an agile animal with short front legs.

ORNITHISCHIANS

Ornithischians were also originally bipedal, but, unlike the first Saurischians, they were vegetarian. They all showed greater development of the hind limbs than the forelimbs, although some later adopted a mainly quadrupedal way of moving. One early group of Ornithischians were called ornithopods, a reference to the bird-like shape of the hind foot. *Heterodontosaurus* was an example. It was small and agile, and had specialized teeth for chewing vegetation thoroughly. It is possible that it shed and replaced its worn teeth while aestivating (resting up) during the dry season. It also had tusks to defend itself against the threat of predators.

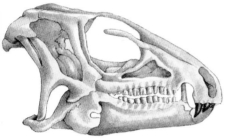

ABOVE *The fossil skull of* Heterodontosaurus *shows differentiated teeth. Each side of the lower jaw was in three sections, with moveable joints between. The middle sections moved in and out as the animal chewed.*

During the Mesozoic era the dinosaurs developed to fill every land-based ecological niche available. They survived on the tough conifers and tree ferns of the forests, the myriad insects, and other small creatures that lived amongst the plants, and on meat provided by the herbivores. They were already a very diverse group of animals with very different characteristics. We can no longer think of an idealized "dinosaur," but a whole range of animals which were as different in their appearances and habits as they were in size.

Another early Ornithischian was described by Richard Owen in 1859. *Scelidosaurus* was a small, armored reptile from the early part of the Jurassic period. It was a heavily-built animal, with spines along its back, but its exact relationship to the later armored dinosaurs is unclear.

Heterodontosaurus

PLANT-EATERS

SAUROPODS

The early prosauropods already had the main features of a typical sauropod, or "reptile-footed," dinosaur. They were mainly quadrupedal, although many could rear up on their hind legs. They were vegetarian, and had long necks to reach up for the foliage of shrubs and trees; the long tail probably acted as a counterbalance. They had long, clawed or hoofed toes and fingers, and lizard-like serrated teeth.

From this group the true sauropods appeared, establishing themselves by the end of the Jurassic period (see *Diplodocus*). The main development was in size. They became larger throughout their evolution, and larger, and larger …

The sauropod nostrils migrated during their evolution, from the normal position near the end of the snout to the top of the small head, between the eyes. The reason for this is unclear. It was once thought that these dinosaurs were aquatic animals, and the nostrils on the top of the head worked like a skin-diver's snorkel. However, the design of the rest of the body would not have suited a deep-water existence. The rib cage could not have been strong enough to prevent lung

collapse and heart failure, due to the extra pressure of deep water.

However, sauropod footprints have been found which suggest that they did spend time wading in water. The footprints indicate that the animal walked along the bottom of a lake using its front legs only, as the rest of the body floated. The track turns

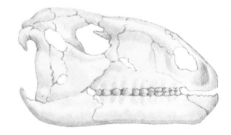

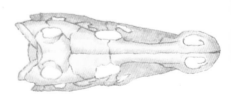

ABOVE *The skull of the Ornithischian ornithopod* Tenontosaurus *shows that its teeth were designed for chewing, something that the Saurischian sauropods were not good at. It also had cheeks to prevent the food being lost during chewing.* Tenontosaurus *was not as large as the sauropods, since it may not have needed a huge fermentation vat for a stomach.*

sharply where the print of a hind foot suggests it kicked against the mud. It is likely, therefore, that these animals may well have lived near water, wading and swimming as necessary in search of aquatic vegetation, or to escape predators.

Typical sauropod legs were strong, weight-bearing pillars. They were capable of only limited movement, much like our land giant of today, the elephant. They had short, stumpy fingers and toes, only one or two of which bore claws – the others being "hoofed" or "nailed," again like an elephant's. As the sauropods became bigger, the front legs grew more lengthy in proportion to the hind legs – indeed, the gigantic *Brachiosaurus* is named for its long "arms."

Most of the sauropods had extraordinarily long necks, the longest of which so far discovered was that of *Mamenchisaurus* (36 ft).

It is widely accepted that the long sauropod neck was an adaptation for reaching high vegetation; it may also have been used in the water to collect lake-bed plants. It seems unlikely that the biggest sauropods could have spent long with their necks in the tree-tops, because today's evidence from comparative anatomy and physiology tells us that pumping blood so high to the brain would have been impossible for a normal reptilian heart. If these creatures did browse in the high branches all day, then they must have had a more advanced type of heart, with fully divided chambers – which occur only in mammals and birds today. (This is one strand of the argument for dinosaur warm-bloodedness.)

Although to us it may seem eccentric and primitive, the sauropod design was obviously successful. It persisted with only minor variations for more than 140 million years.

Mamenchisaurus

FLESH-EATERS

Meat is a very rich food, containing virtually all of the nutrients needed for energy and growth. Consequently meat-eaters, or carnivores, do not need to eat as much, or as often, as herbivores. Modern crocodiles can survive for months after a big meal! Meat is also easy to digest. It can be broken down easily by chemicals produced by the vertebrate digestive system; no special grinding or fermenting equipment is necessary.

Compared to plants, however, meat is more difficult to obtain. It tends to run away. Herbivores do not need to be speedy or agile to obtain their

ABOVE *The jawbone of* Allosaurus *was very deep, indicating powerful jaw muscles used to hold prey. The teeth are also ideal for a carnivore; being serrated, they were efficient at tearing flesh, while the backwards curve allowed them to securely grip a struggling animal.*

meals – although they may have these attributes to escape from predators. Carnivores must be able to catch, kill, and cut up their prey. They tend to be active animals equipped with good sensory facilities, a degree of sophisticated hunting behavior or "cunning," and weapons for killing and dismembering their food. This applies across the animal kingdom, from a dragonfly to a pike to a tiger – and a dinosaur.

The carnivorous dinosaurs belonged to the same group as the sauropods, the Saurischians. The first one to be discovered, indeed the first dinosaur scientifically named, was *Megalosaurus*, found in Oxfordshire in the nineteenth century.

Like the ancestors of the Saurischians, the carnivorous dinosaurs were all active, bipedal animals, well armed with claws and teeth. Some of them, the theropods, reached huge sizes, although none as large as the great sauropods. They needed to be big, partly because they fed on these even bigger herbivores.

These large hunters had big heads with sizeable eyes and fearsome teeth. Their necks were thick and powerful, their front legs small and sometimes apparently useless. They walked on powerful hind legs, using the long tail

Allosaurus

for counterbalance. Fingers and toes bore claws but were often reduced in number. This general description, however, hides the many variations in the behavior and lifestyle of these fearsome carnivores.

Allosaurus was a fine example of a carnosaur, one of the groups of theropod meat-eaters. It shows the features and habits similar in all members of the group. However this particular animal was large, and perhaps too bulky to move at speed over any distance, although it could have been stealthy and agile when close to its prey. In any case, the large sauropods and stegosaurs on which it fed were not fast-moving themselves. They were more susceptible to ambush.

Some hunting dinosaurs may well have operated in groups or packs which could have brought down even the largest of the plant-eaters. But like modern predators, such as lions and wolves, it would be more economical in terms of energy to take young or sick victims from the herds. There is little doubt that they would have also taken advantage of any carrion by scavenging.

EGG-STEALERS AND INSECT-SNATCHERS

Some dinosaur carnivores concentrated on the vast walking meals which were the huge sauropods and other large herbivores of their time. Other groups of carnivores, such as the lightly-built coelurosaurs and the ostrich dinosaurs, took advantage of smaller prey. They avoided the problems of battling with and overcoming large herbivorous prey, and concentrated on the little creatures that shared their world.

Insects and other arthropods, such as scorpions and millipedes, were well established on the land by the time of the dinosaurs. In fact, they had been among the first creatures to colonize the land, and had already been evolving for 200 million years. Although their fossils are rare, the animals were probably as common as they are today, if not more so. They would have been an important part of the ecological food web, positioned between plants and the larger carnivores.

Another new and important food source was provided by shelled eggs, laid by dinosaurs and most other reptiles, as well as by the newly-

evolving birds. These eggs, deposited on land, must have been vulnerable to any animal quick enough to avoid the protective parent or to find them hidden away in a hole or nest.

CERATOSAURS

The ceratosaurs were an early dinosaur group. Their fossils appear in the lower layers of Triassic rocks. The early representatives were unspecialized predators, apparently eating anything they could catch. *Coelophysis*, one of the first, has been found with the remains of young of the same species within the stomach area. Too well developed to be unborn

Coelophysis

embryos, could these be evidence of the last meal of a cannibal?

COELUROSAURS

One of the smallest dinosaurs so far found and fully described, *Compsognathus*, was a coelurosaur. One specimen had eaten a small, fast-moving lizard for its final feast, judging by the fossilized bones found within its own body area. The coelurosaur group continued successfully throughout the Mesozoic era, with members becoming more specialized as they developed.

ORNITHOMIMOSAURS

The ostrich dinosaurs, or ornithomimosaurs, are named for their resemblance – in both shape and habits – to the modern ostrich-type birds. These dinosaurs were a group of theropods which appeared in the Cretaceous period.

Several of their members, such as *Struthiomimus* and *Gallimimus*, have provoked varied theories for their diet and feeding behaviors. The main

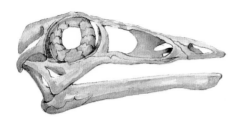

ABOVE *Many fossils originally described as* Ornithomimus *were later assigned to* Struthiomimus, *shown here. The animals were very similar, but come from different areas. The skull of* Struthiomimus *shows many parallels to birds: a toothless beak, large eye sockets, and delicate bones are all common features.*

features of the group includes a toothless beak, long arms, and fingers, very long and slim but muscular legs, bird-like feet, and a short, counterbalancing tail. One suggestion is that they were wading seashore animals living on small shrimps, winkles, and other shellfish, which they found by flicking over pebbles. They might have been "anteaters," although their hands and arms were not well developed for digging. Or they were possibly herbivores, reaching vegetation with the long arms and neck, and stripping leaves from their stems with the beak.

But the most likely interpretation so far is that these animals were omnivores which, like the ostrich today, would eat virtually any food – seeds, fruits, insects, and small mammals and other little creatures – that they could find. The adaptable "beak" and long fingers may have been capable of manipulating seeds and nuts out of their husks.

The skeletons of these animals do indeed show remarkable similarities to those of ostriches. They were adapted for speed. The head, neck, and body were counterbalanced by the tail. This was usually held straight, but could be moved from side to side to balance the animal as it turned sharply when on the move. The long bones of the legs were hollow, to lighten their weight and reduce the momentum as they swung with each stride.

The feet were very similar to those of ostriches, with long toes providing a good grip of the ground when running. Comparisons show that most ostrich dinosaurs must have been so swift that they could outrun enemies, and also catch low-flying insects or quick-moving lizards and other small vertebrates.

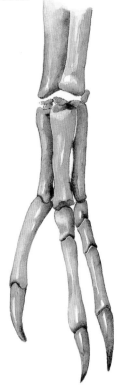

ABOVE *The hand of* Struthiomimus *had slim and delicate bones. There were only three clawed fingers, but this theropod could probably grasp small items when the animal was searching for fruit or insects.*

OVIRAPTORS

Oviraptors were a specialized group of theropods whose likely lifestyle was as egg-stealers (as their name suggests). *Oviraptor* had a short, toothless beak with a short tusk on the end of the upper jaw. The jaw bones and muscle-anchorage scars suggest that the animal had a powerful bite, probably strong enough to crush eggshells. And the first *Oviraptor* fossil ever found was lying over a clutch of *Protoceratops* eggs – very compelling evidence of their lifestyle! The animal could have been literally "caught in the act" by the processes of fossilization.

Oviraptor had more specialized hands than coelurosaurs or ostrich dinosaurs, with three fingers on each, bearing curved claws. The skeletons of these animals also had a "wishbone" in the chest made of the fused collarbones. Birds have fused collarbones, too. It is thought that their origins may well lie among the ancestors of this group of dinosaurs, although not oviraptors themselves, because birds such as *Archaeopteryx* had been around for 70 million years before the *Oviraptor* appeared.

HORNS AND ARMOR

CERATOPIANS

The dinosaur world was swarming with predators that overcame their prey either by great bulk and power, or by swiftness and agility. One means of defense against their teeth and claws was to be protected by hard, tough shields, plates, nodules, lumps, spikes, spines, and other kinds of armor. The ceratopian dinosaurs and their kin adopted these devices, and in typical dinosaur tradition, carried it to extremes.

The ceratopians were likely descendants of creatures similar to *Psittacosaurus* (see page 68).

BELOW *The skeleton of a* Triceratops. *There were probably several species of the* Triceratops *genus, differing mainly in size.*

Protoceratops appeared after *Psittacosaurus* in the fossil record. Although only the size of a large dog, this dinosaur had already lost its bipedal stance. The increasing size of its skull in proportion to the body, together with the frill appearing over the neck, meant that the front of the body needed the support of front legs.

The neck frill may have developed originally as a bony anchorage flange for the great muscles needed to operate the jaws. *Protoceratops'* cheek-teeth were arranged in batteries and formed scissor-like blades, which chopped plant material.

An insight into ceratopian family life has been provided by fossil finds of eggs and young. The differences between males and females indicate a

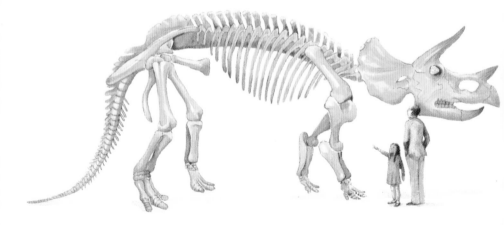

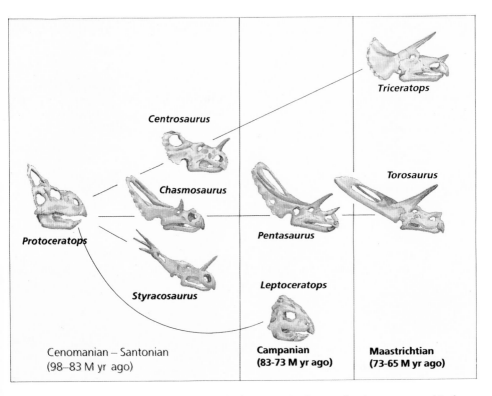

| Cenomanian – Santonian (98–83 M yr ago) | Campanian (83-73 M yr ago) | Maastrichtian (73-65 M yr ago) |

structured society, with males perhaps fighting over, and then protecting, the females and their young.

Up to 20 eggs were laid, their more pointed ends down, in concentric circles in a hollow in the sand. Some fossilized eggs have been found to contain embryo dinosaurs, while certain nests also contain hatchlings.

Continued evolution of the ceratopian group produced much larger animals, with even more elaborate head and neck

ABOVE *Ceratopian horns seemed to have been for defense initially, thereafter developing as social and sexual features. At first the neck frill was an extension of the bones at the back of the skull, for the attachment of the large jaw muscles, thereafter developing for protection. From Protoceratops, which had a small frill and nose ridge, these characteristics followed different lines of evolution.*

embellishments. The skull enlarged in proportion to the body. The first three vertebral bones, in the neck, became fused to support the massive weight of the head. The neck frills got larger – and horns appeared.

Centrosaurus had a small neck frill with "windows" for the attachment of jaw muscles, but *Triceratops* had a longer frill which had lost the windows. This beast also had one nose horn and two brow horns. This frill seems less for the attachment of jaw muscles, and social behavior, than for defense against the tyrannosaurs of the time.

The frills got even larger. *Torosaurus* was the record-holder, with the biggest skull of virtually any land vertebrate. It lived right at the end of the Cretaceous period, and its frill had only small windows and no notable decorations. There were three horns on its face, those on the brow being as much as 5 ft long when covered with the horny sheath.

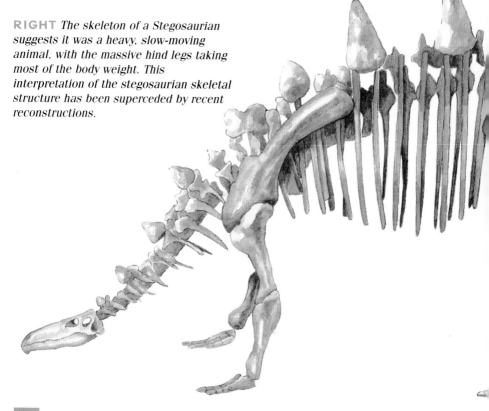

RIGHT *The skeleton of a Stegosaurian suggests it was a heavy, slow-moving animal, with the massive hind legs taking most of the body weight. This interpretation of the stegosaurian skeletal structure has been superceded by recent reconstructions.*

STEGOSAURS

The stegosaurs were another group of Ornithischian dinosaurs, which appeared long before the ceratopians. They had also returned to using four feet for locomotion. These herbivores varied greatly in size, and they are famous as the dinosaurs with huge bony plates arranged along the back.

Typical stegosaur features included a small head held close to the ground on a short neck, weak jaws with small cheek teeth (they may have relied on

ABOVE *The splayed spines on the tail end of the* Stegosaurus *would have been effective weapons as the tail thrashed from side to side.*

stomach stones and large fermenting gut-chambers to aid digestion), short but strong front legs, and longer hind legs. They had elephant-like feet with hoofed toes. The tail was short for a dinosaur, and ended with several bony spikes – the only apparent means of defense. The vertebrae and ribs were very large, in order to support the great weight of the animal.

Stegosaurs in general, and *Stegosaurus* in particular, are noted for the very small size of the brain in proportion to the body. *Stegosaurus* also had an enlargement of the spinal cord in its hip region, often called a "second brain." In fact, the brain in the skull was probably adequate for its placid, browsing existence; the enlargement in the hips may merely have been the place where all the nerves of the legs and tail entered the spinal cord.

Casts of the insides of *Stegosaurus* skulls indicate that the brain of this creature probably weighed less than 3½ oz. With a body weight of some 1½ tons, this gives a body:brain ratio of 15,000:1. In ourselves, the same ratio is about 50:1. Yet stegosaurs survived for tens of millions of years, so evidently the attributes of a large brain were not important in its world.

NODOSAURS AND ANKYLOSAURS

The nodosaurs and ankylosaurs are two further groups of Ornithischian dinosaurs that developed the armor theme. They were not particularly large dinosaurs, but their skin was covered with various patterns of bony nodules, plates, and spines – they were truly armored dinosaurs.

Built along the same lines as the ceratopians, they had small heads which were heavily plated with extra bone. There was a bony palate between the mouth and nasal cavity,

an unusual feature for a reptile, which allowed the animal to breathe and chew at the same time. This was taken even further in the ankylosaurs, which had long nasal passages associated with well-developed olfactory lobes (smell centers) in the brain. They may have used their powerful sense of smell to search for food or avoid predators.

The bony nodules of *Nodosaurus* functioned rather like a coarse chain-mail suit, providing protection and flexibility. *Polacanthus* (a nodosaur) and *Ankylosaurus* had spikes, and the latter possessed a massive club at the end of its stiffened tail – a supremely effective defensive weapon.

These animals were not large, and were probably fairly agile compared to the huge meat-eating theropods. As a last resort, when being attacked, they may have crouched close to the ground, thereby being very awkward to tip up or turn over. The attacker, its teeth slipping and scrabbling on the back armor, may have given up in favor of easier prey. The same sort of defensive behavior is seen in some modern-day creatures, such as the hedgehog or the echidna. If it came to an open fight, the tail club of an ankylosaur could easily have floored a bipedal theropod, perhaps breaking its leg at the same time – in the same way that a small child, being forced into action, might kick a larger one in the shin before running off!

Polacanthus

Nodosaurus

PACHYCEPHALOSAURS

The pachycephalosaurs were another group of Ortnithischians, from late in the Age of Dinosaurs. They had not lost their bipedal stance and retained teeth at the front of their jaws. They were mostly smallish, although *Pachycephalosaurus* itself reached the size of a large horse.

These dinosaurs were grazing animals and may have lived as sheep and goats do today. They had no armor except for an immensely strengthened skull dome, with the bone being up to 10 in thick in *Pachycephalosaurus*, and small bony knobs and horns surrounding it. It has been suggested that these "dome-heads" or "thick-heads" may have defended themselves, their territories, mates, or offspring,

by a display of head-butting – as rams do nowadays. The fact that the head was held at an angle to the spine, unlike other dinosaurs, and the bones of the neck were thickened and closely jointed to absorb shock, are further evidence for this feature of their lifestyle.

Pachycephalosaurus

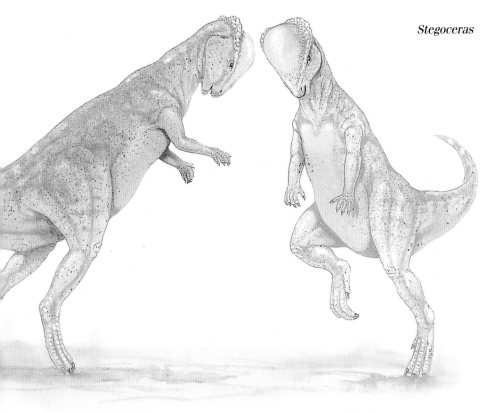

Stegoceras

RIGHT *Pachycephalosaur remains are rare fossils, these dinosaurs being known only by their teeth for half a century. More recent finds include several skull fragments, but little of the body skeleton. This is the skull of* Prenocephale, *which lived about 70 million years ago. The animal was some 7 ft long, and its fossils come from North America.*

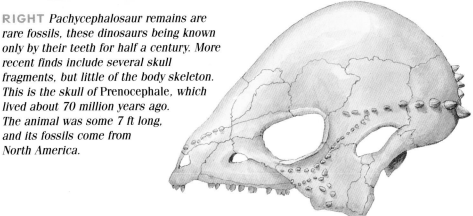

LIZARD-TEETH AND DUCK-BILLS

The last main groups of Ornithischians in our dinosaur survey are the iguanodontids and hadrosaurs. They were thought to be closely related, both being bipedal herbivores that reached medium-to-large sizes. They had multipurpose hands and, as they evolved, fossils indicate that there was increased adaptation toward a social way of life.

An early iguanodontid, *Camptosaurus*, appeared at the end of the Jurassic period, some 150 million years ago. It seems that the group replaced the giant sauropods as the main herbivores around this time, and they continued as such throughout the Cretaceous period. Their appearance

Iguanadon

and diversification in the fossil record corresponds approximately to the evolution of flowering plants, and this new food source may have contributed to their diet.

The hadrosaurs did not evolve until later, about 100 million years ago. They were becoming ever more specialized and diversified when the Age of Dinosaurs was suddenly terminated, 65 million years ago.

IGUANODONTIDS

Iguanodon was one of the first dinosaurs to be discovered to science, and its fossils were extensively studied when the science of palaeontology was in its infancy. Fossilized teeth, and later bones, were found by Gideon Mantell in the early 1820s. He went to great lengths to discover what sort of animal they came from and he eventually realized that the teeth were similar, although much larger, to those of the living iguana lizard. He therefore named his creature *Iguanodon* ("iguana tooth"), and published a description and reconstruction of the animal.

Since that time many complete specimens of *Iguanodon* have been found across Europe and Asia. It is probably one of the most studied of all dinosaurs, and much has been conjectured about its appearance and lifestyle. However, this extensive body

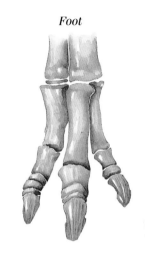

Foot

ABOVE/BELOW *The foot of* Iguanodon *had three strong, widely splayed toes. The three middle fingers of the hand could support some weight when necessary, while the thumb spike and little finger may have been used for manipulating food.*

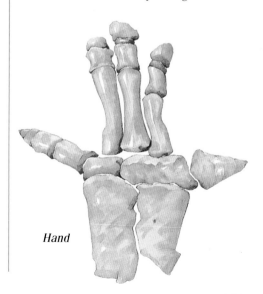

Hand

of knowledge and guesswork serves to illustrate how much we will never know about life in the past – very little can be gleaned about the beast's internal anatomy of soft tissues such as the gut, excretory, and reproductive organs, and virtually nothing about the metabolism. Suggestions have been made by various scientists concerning the ecology and behavior of these animals, based on studies of the fossilized teeth and bones, and also on the circumstantial evidence of which fossils have been found together, but these will of necessity remain educated proposals.

Ouranosaurus was a similar animal to *Iguanodon*, although it lived slightly later. Its vertebral spines were elongated to form the supports for a skin "sail" that rain down the back, between the shoulders and the end of the tail. Richly supplied with blood vessels, this was probably a temperature-regulating device as with the back plates of Stegosaurus, and very handy for an animal that lived in equatorial extremes of climate.

HADROSAURS

Hadrosaurs appeared towards the end of the Cretaceous period. The evidence points to them taking over ecological roles from iguanodontids wherever their geographical ranges overlapped, as in North America and Asia. They never reached western Europe, however, and the iguanodontids continued there until the end of the Age of Dinosaurs.

The typical hadrosaur body shape and size was similar to the iguanodontids. Their main innovations were in and on the head, and were concerned with food processing and social behavior.

Hadrosaurs are commonly called "duckbilled dinosaurs" for the duck-like bill which characterized the group. The front of the jaw formed a widely splayed "beak," rather than the much narrower bill of the iguanodontids. Many rows of cheek teeth were cemented together to form rasping surfaces, for extra effectiveness in the never-ending task of crushing tough plant material. In fact, remains of the plants they ate – flowering and non-flowering trees and shrubs – have been preserved with some of the fossils.

The hands had only four fingers, the thumb (with its spike) having been lost. Hadrosaur hands were sometimes paddle-shaped, and together with the deep tail, this suggests that they could swim when necessary. Swimming was perhaps their only means of defense, because they otherwise seemed to lack armor or natural weapons.

The early hadrosaurs had various modifications to the front of the skull and nasal passages. Some had bumps on their noses, while others such as

Edmontosaurus could probably inflate skin sacks, perhaps for visual display and vocalization, as in certain seals and some birds today.

In the best dinosaur tradition, these early adaptations were carried to extremes in other hadrosaurs. Strange crests, pipes, tubes, and other projections appeared as headgear. These dinosaurs had big eyes and functional ear bones, so it is likely that the head adornments were used for visual and auditory signalling between individuals of a community.

One of the simpler designs was that of *Saurolophus*. It had a ridge on the top of the skull, and probably bore a fleshy, inflatable bag on the front of its face, connected to the nostrils. The most extreme development was found in *Parasaurolophus*, which had a long, curved crest on the top of its skull. This was hollow and connected to the nasal passages. There is good evidence that the crest was larger in males than in females of this dinosaur, and the likely conclusion is that this extraordinary "topknot" was connected with courtship displays and/or territorial behavior.

BELOW *Parasaurolophus lived during the late Cretaceous period. Nasal passages passed from the nostrils, inside and up to the top of the crest, then down to the throat and lungs. This long tube may have been used as a "trumpet" for vocal communication. The female skull is sectioned to show the shorter nasal passage which would have made a higher-pitched noise.*

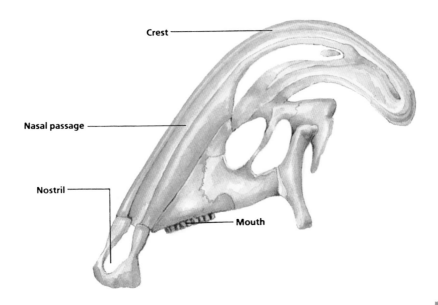

Crest

Nasal passage

Nostril

Mouth

HOW TO USE THE IDENTIFIER

This section is laid out so as to provide a concise and clear guide to identifying dinosaurs. The A–Z identifier section consists of individual entries for each kind of dinosaur. Each entry is illustrated and gives concise details of classification, its size, its age, and its particular traits and characteristics. The symbols accompanying each entry convey the essential details at a glance.

AGE

Triassic
(245–208 million years ago)

Jurassic
(208–144 million years ago)

Cretaceous (144–65 million years ago)

**MEASUREMENTS
(IN FEET)**

Height

Length

EATING HABIT

Carnivore

Herbivore

Omnivore

DINOSAUR IDENTIFIER

ALBERTOSAURUS

Classification Order Saurischia, Suborder Theropoda
Age Late Cretaceous, 70 million years ago
Measurements Height 13 ft, length 29½ ft
Fossil sites USA (Alberta)
Notes This dinosaur, a close relative of *Tyrannosaurus*, is named after its discovery site. It was lightly-built and could have actively hunted prey such as hadrosaurs, rather than waiting for them to die from other causes as the larger carnivores did.

ALLOSAURUS

Classification Order Saurischia, Suborder Theropoda
Age Late Jurassic, 150 million years ago
Measurements Height 16½ ft, length 39 ft
Fossil sites USA (Colorado), Africa, Australia
Notes *Allosaurus* means "strange reptile". Its skull was more than 3 ft long and its

jaws were lined with serrated, back-curved teeth. The teeth pointed towards the throat so that flesh, once bitten, could not slip out of the jaws, nor a struggling victim pull itself free. Unlike *Tyrannosaurus*, this dinosaur had strong front legs with sharp claws on the fingers. It walked on its back legs, which were strong and well-clawed but not designed for speed.

It had many cavities in its skull to reduce its weight. The muscles connected with the jaws would have been large and powerful, and the jaw itself was hinged far back on the skull, to allow a huge gape.

Like its cousins, *Allosaurus* had a short, strong neck. This is even more extreme in *Tyrannosaurus*. The powerful neck not only supported the heavy skull but also allowed the animal to twist and pull its head, as it tore and wrenched lumps of flesh from its victim. *Allosaurus* had bony hollows above its eyes, which could have held salt-glands to remove excess salt from the body. Many living animals, such as seabirds and crocodiles, have similar hollows.

16½   39

ANCHISAURUS

Classification Order Saurischia, Suborder
Sauropodomorpha
Age Early Jurassic, 200 million years ago
Measurements Height about 2 ft,
length 8 ft
Fossil sites Eastern North America

Notes *Anchisaurus* means "close reptile."
This was a lightly-built early prosauropod
which could stand on two legs or four. It
had pencil-like teeth spaced along its jaw
and ate vegetation.

ANKYLOSAURUS

Classification Order Ornithischia, Suborder Ankylosauria
Age Late Cretaceous, 70 million years ago
Measurements Height about 10 ft, Length 33 ft
Fossil sites North America
Notes *Ankylosaurus* means "fused reptile" and refers to the fused body elements of the armor-plating. It was one of the largest dinosaurs of the ankylosaur group. The bony plates in the skin are enlarged and fused, both together and to the end bones of the tail. This huge bony club, at the end of an otherwise flexible and powerful tail, would have been an effective defense. The ankylosaur could easily have damaged a tyrannosaur's legs, rendering it helpless.

10   33

APATOSAURUS

Classification Order Saurischia, Suborder Sauropodomorpha
Age Late Jurassic, 150 million years ago
Measurements Height 23 ft, length 69 ft, weight 30 tons
Fossil sites North America
Notes This name means "deceptive reptile" because there was much confusion about its evolutionary relationships when it was discovered. Like the other diplodocids, *Apatosaurus* must have fed virtually continuously on plants, either on the ground or in trees. It pulled off leaves with its peg-like teeth and swallowed them whole. Its stomach contained pebbles which the animal had swallowed, to grind up the plant material.

  23 69

BRACHIOSAURUS

Classification Order Saurischia, Suborder Sauropodomorpha
Age Jurassic, 150 million years ago
Measurements Height about 39 ft, length 74 ft, weight 50 tons

Fossil sites USA (Colorado), Africa, Europe
Notes This "arm reptile" although not the longest dinosaur, was one of the heaviest. It was able to browse on the leaves at the tops of trees because of its long neck and long front legs, like a giant giraffe. Its nostrils were placed high on its forehead. At one time it was thought the nostril position indicated a snorkeling underwater existence, but there are no other obvious aquatic features, so this is unlikely. The reason for the position of the nostrils is still unclear.

39   74

CAMPTOSAURUS

Classification Order Ornithischia,
Suborder Ornithopoda
Age Late Jurassic, 150 million years ago
Measurements Height 12 ft,
length 16–23 ft
Fossil sites North America, Europe
Notes *Camptosaurus* means "flexible
reptile." It was a medium iguanodon-type
dinosaur which appeared early in the
group's evolution. It still had four toes on
its back feet and no thumb-spike, but
otherwise it was very similar to *Iguanodon*.

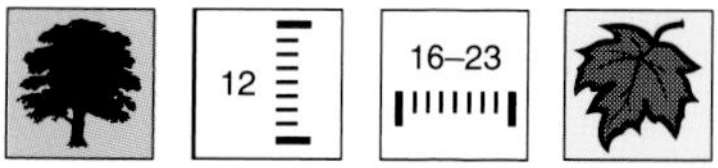

12

16–23

CENTROSAURUS

Classification Order Ornithischia, Suborder Ceratopia
Age Late Cretaceous, 75 million years ago
Measurements Height 8 ft, length 20 ft
Fossil sites North America
Notes *Centrosaurus* means "sharp point reptile." This animal had one nose horn, and its neck frill was edged with spines, two of which pointed down towards the face. It probably lived in small herds, the males defending the females and young.

  8 20

COELOPHYSIS

Classification Order Saurischia, Suborder Theropoda
Age Triassic, 220 million years ago
Measurements Height about 4 ft, length 10 ft, lightly built
Fossil sites North America
Notes *Coelophysis* means "hollow form." It was one of the earliest dinosaurs. A fast-moving bipedal animal that ate small creatures such as insects and reptiles. It had long, narrow jaws with many sharp, serrated teeth, and the front limbs ended in grasping hands.

DEINONYCHUS

Classification Order Saurischia, Suborder Theropoda
Age Cretaceous, 100 million years ago
Measurements Height 5½ ft, length 10 ft
Fossil sites USA (Montana)
Notes *Deinonychus* means "terrible claw" and accurately describes the sickle-shaped claw on the second toe of each foot. These smallish, slim animals were designed for speed, and the tail was used as a

counterbalance. It could be held out rigidly when the animal was running, or flexed to allow for sudden cornering. These animals probably hunted in packs and could tackle the large sauropods of the time.

  5½ 10

DILOPHOSAURUS

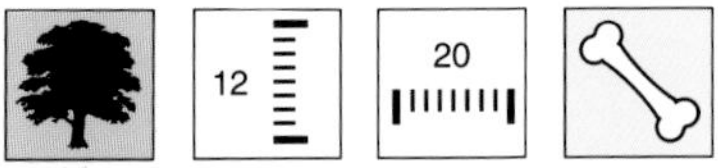

Classification Order Saurischia, Suborder Theropoda
Age Jurassic, 190 million years ago
Measurements Height about 12 ft, length 20 ft
Fossil sites USA (Arizona), China
Notes *Dilophosaurus* means "ridged reptile." This bipedal dinosaur had two ridges running along its face, between the eyes. These bony features were paper-thin but had thickened struts for support. They were probably involved with the mating behavior of the animals, perhaps distinguishing males from females and used for display.

12

20

DIPLODOCUS

Classification Order Saurischia, Suborder Sauropodomorpha
Age Jurassic, 145 million years ago
Measurements Height about 30 ft, length 89 ft, weight 10–11 tons
Fossil sites North America
Notes *Diplodocus* means "double beam," reflecting the cantilever arrangement of the neck, tail, and body. One of the longest known dinosaurs – most of the length being neck and tail – this animal was a slimly-built, lightweight version of the giant plant-eaters. It also had its nostrils on the top of its head. There was only one claw on each front foot, but probably two on each hind foot. Some specimens show evidence for a wedge of tissue under the foot, forming a heel to improve walking ability.

Their jaws were feeble and must have served only for stripping leaves from branches, perhaps with a raking motion. The leaves were then swallowed whole. There was little or no chewing apparatus – *Diplodocus* had only a fringe of thin teeth at the front of its fragile jaws, and the muscle-anchorage scars on the tiny skull and jaw bones show that the muscles here were small and weak.

  30 89

EDMONTOSAURUS

Classification Order Ornithischia, Suborder Ornithopoda
Age Late Cretaceous, 65 million years ago
Measurements Height 9½ ft, length 33–42 ft
Fossil sites North America
Notes *Edmontosaurus* is named for the place it was first found, Edmonton, Canada. The jaws of this hadrosaur formed the characteristic toothless "duck-bill" at the front, while at the back were several hundred grinding teeth, arranged as flat rasping surfaces, that moved past each other as the animal chewed. These could certainly deal with tough vegetation. The animal also had paddle-like hands and a deep tail, perhaps for an escape swim when the land-based carnivorous dinosaurs threatened. These dinosaurs were social animals, nesting in colonies. Maybe they signaled to each other with an inflatable skin sack on the top of the nose, which could have made extremely loud sounds, similar to those made by the howler monkey's throat pouch.

9½   33–42

GALLIMIMUS

Classification Order Saurischia, Suborder Theropoda
Age Late Cretaceous, 70 million years ago
Measurements Height about 9 ft, length 20 ft
Fossil sites Mongolia
Notes *Gallimimus* means "chicken mimic." These bipedal dinosaurs were slim and swift, members of the ostrich dinosaur group, and they had many features in common with early birds. They had toothless beak-like jaws, large eyes, powerful back legs, and a stiff, counter-balancing tail. They were probably omnivores, catching whatever small creatures they could, and gathering suitable vegetation with the long arms.

HETERODONTOSAURUS

Classification Order Ornithischia, Suborder Ornithopoda
Age Jurassic, 200 million years ago
Measurements Height about 2 ft, length 4 ft
Fossil sites South Africa
Notes *Heterodontosaurus* means "mixed tooth reptile." It had chisel-shaped teeth at the front of its jaw, tusks and broad ridged the front of its jaw, tusks and broad ridged teeth at the back. An early type of dinosaur, this bipedal animal's well differentiated teeth and jaws could deal with various foods. It was well equipped to deal with the tough plants on which it lived, and its main defense against predators was probably speed of escape.

IGUANODON

Classification Order Ornithischia, Suborder Ornithopoda
Age Cretaceous, 120 million years ago
Measurements Height 16 ft, length 30 ft
Fossil sites Europe, North Africa, and Asia
Notes *Iguanodon* is one of the first- and best-studied of dinosaurs, named for the resemblance of its teeth to those of an iguana. It was a large plant-eating animal which could stand on its hind legs. It had a large thumb-spike for raking together vegetation or for defense; the little finger was flexible and may have been used to manipulate food; while the three middle fingers were robust and hoofed for walking on all fours.

The mechanism of chewing was novel and may have been responsible for the success of these animals. The teeth in the upper jaw came down slightly to the outside of the lower teeth, rather than straight down on to them. As the teeth came together the bones of the upper jaw probably moved apart slightly, so that the working surfaces of the teeth could grind across each other. The food was contained in cheek pouches, just as in ourselves, so that it could be repeatedly remashed and reground, before being swallowed.

Iguanodon's brain was large, for a reptile, and it seems that these animals had well-developed senses. They could have been capable of the learning and reasoning processes necessary for social behavior and care of the young.

  16 30

MAIASAURA

Classification Order Ornithischia, Suborder Ornithopoda
Age Late Cretaceous, 80 million years ago
Measurements Height 9 ft, length 30 ft
Fossil sites North America
Notes *Maiasaura*, "good mother reptile," refers to the supposed behavior of the parents, from evidence of eggs and baby hadrosaurs found fossilized in their nests.

The babies were 20–40 in long, while larger young with worn teeth were found near the nests. It seems that the animals nested in colonies, returning to the same site every year, and bringing their other youngsters. The mother laid about 20 eggs, and she or some combinations of adults raised the young and supplied them with food.

MAMENCHISAURUS

Classification Order Saurischia, Suborder Sauropodomorpha

Age Jurassic, 150 million years ago

Measurements Height about 30 ft, length 82 ft

Fossil sites China

Notes The animal is named for the place it was first discovered, Mamenchi. The extraordinary neck accounts for nearly half of the total body length, and it is the longest-necked dinosaur so far discovered. The bone structure indicates that it was not a particularly flexible neck, despite its length.

  30 82

MEGALOSAURUS

Classification Order Saurischia, Suborder Theropoda
Age Jurassic, 160 million years ago
Measurements Height 9½ ft, length 23–26 ft, weight 2 tons
Fossil sites England, France
Notes *Megalosaurus* means "big reptile" and it was another of the carnosaurs that preyed on the large plant-eating dinosaurs of the time. This animal was one of the first dinosaurs to be given a scientific name. Its remains are incomplete; many fragments of the theropod skeletons have been identified as being of *Megalosaurus* in the past, but further work is suggesting that they are from a variety of theropods.

9½   23–26

NODOSAURUS

Classification Order Ornithischia, Suborder Ankylosauria
Age Cretaceous, 80 million years ago
Measurements Height 6 ft, length 18 ft
Fossil sites North America
Notes *Nodosaurus* means "lumpy reptile" and refers to the armoring on the skin. There were rows of bony nodules, alternately large and small, arranged across the back, neck, and tail. These animals must have protected themselves by crouching low to the ground like an armadillo, presenting only the upper armored surface to an attacker, with their shape and weight making them difficult to turn over.

  6 18

59

ORNITHOMIMUS

Classification Order Saurischia, Suborder Theropoda
Age Late Cretaceous, 75 million years ago
Measurements Height 7 ft, length 13 ft
Fossil sites Western USA
Notes *Ornithomimus*, or "speedy bird mimic," was smaller than *Gallimimus*, but

almost certainly closely related and also led a similar omnivorous lifestyle – even though their fossils are half a world apart.

OURANOSAURUS

Classification Order Ornithischia,
Suborder Ornithopoda
Age Cretaceous, 110 million years ago
Measurements Height 13¼ ft,
length 23 ft
Fossil sites North Africa
Notes *Ouranosaurus*, the "brave reptile,"
was an iguanodontid that lived in an

equatorial climate. The sail of skin
stretched over backbone spines was
probably used for temperature regulation.

  13¼ 23

OVIRAPTOR

Classification Order Saurischia, Suborder Therapoda
Age Late Cretaceous, 80 million years ago
Measurements Height 4¼ ft, length 5–6½ ft
Fossil sites Mongolia
Notes *Oviraptor* was the original "egg thief." The heavy, toothless beak, with a horny covering in life, was probably used to break open the eggs of other dinosaurs (or birds) so that it could consume the contents. It had three long, clawed fingers on each hand, and ran like an ostrich or emu on its hind legs.

4½   5–6½

PACHYCEPHALOSAURUS

Classification Order Ornithischia, Suborder Marginocephalia
Age Late Cretaceous, 70 million years ago
Measurements Height 8 ft, length 15 ft
Fossil sites North America
Notes *Pachycephalosaurus* is the "thick-headed reptile," referring not to its supposed intelligence but to the thick bone of the upper skull. It was the largest of its group and, along with the thickened bones on the top of the skull, there were bony nodules and spines around the dome. The curious shape of the head, together with the arrangement of the neck and back bones, suggests that these animals could hold their bodies straight and horizontal, with the head at a right angle and the face looking straight down. In this posture they engaged in charging and head-butting behavior, possibly connected with territory and courtship disputes as well as defense.

PARASAUROLOPHUS

Classification Order Ornithischia,
Suborder Ornithopoda
Age Late Cretaceous, 80 million years ago
Measurements Height 19 ft, length 33 ft
Fossil sites North America
Notes *Parasaurolophus* means "beside-ridged reptile." It was a bipedal vegetarian, and member of the hadrosaur group. The extraordinary head ridge, much larger in the male than the female, was probably used as a social signaling device between members of the herd. It is thought that the hadrosaurs in general were noisy, social animals.

19

33

PLATEOSAURUS

Classification Order Saurischia, Suborder Sauropodomorpha
Age Late Triassic, 215 million years ago
Measurements Height about 10 ft, length 20 ft
Fossil sites Europe
Notes *Plateosaurus* means "flat reptile." These dinosaurs were the forerunners of the giant plant-eating dinosaurs of the Jurassic. They were bulky animals which could walk on all fours or bipedally. They had small heads, long necks and a heavy tail. They crushed plants with flat, leaf-shaped teeth and were the dominant grazer-browsers of their time. They were probably the first ground-based creatures that could reach the leaves at the tops of tall trees, rising up on its hind legs to reach high vegetation. Their fingers bore large claws, whose likely use was for gathering and raking down branches, as well as being a deterrent to predators.

POLACANTHUS

Classification Order Ornithischia, Suborder Ankylosauria
Age Cretaceous, 120 million years ago
Measurements Height 3¼ ft, length 13 ft
Fossil sites England, USA
Notes The name *Polacanthus,* "like many spikes," refers to the spines that were found at the rear of the skeleton. Few of these dinosaurs have been found in a good state of preservation, so their armor arrangement is not fully understood. This dinosaur appears to have been covered with skin armed with bony nodules over its hip region.

 3¼
 13

PROTOCERATOPS

Classification Order Ornithischia, Suborder Ceratopia
Age Late Cretaceous, 80 million years ago
Measurements Height 2½ ft, length 6 ft
Fossil sites Mongolia, China
Notes *Protoceratops* was named "early horned face" because it was one of the earliest true ceratopians yet discovered. This small, four-legged animal had a frill, but its facial horns were represented only by bony swellings. It is an interesting dinosaur because many examples of the remains of its nests and young have been found.

Protoceratops, unlike its probable ancestors, held its head near the ground; presumably it grazed on low vegetation rather than browsing higher up in shrubs and trees. It did not mash its food; and there is as yet no evidence for stomach stones. Perhaps it was fortunate enough to live among soft, lush, relatively nutritious plant food, that needed little chewing to release its goodness.

Although the attachment of jaw muscles seems to have initiated frill evolution, the reasons for its growth to the extreme sizes seen in the later ceratopian dinosaurs, is a matter for more debate. Analysis of the sizes of many different ceratopian skulls suggests that the frills were larger in males than females. One interpretation is that social behavior and communication were responsible for the development of eccentric frill shapes and sizes. Some modern mammals have adornments such as antlers, horns, tusks, or neck-manes, which signify gender and social position within the group.

PSITTACOSAURUS

Classification Order Ornithischia, Suborder Ceratopia
Age Cretaceous, 100 million years ago
Measurements Height about 4 ft, length 6½ ft
Fossil sites Eastern Asia
Notes *Psittacosaurus* means "parrot reptile", from the parrot-like beak of this animal. It was an early ceratopian and did not possess a neck frill. It had long hind legs and short front limbs with hands. It was a mainly bipedal animal, unlike later members of this group. Some scientists believe it represents a point in evolution between the hadrosaur type of dinosaur and the ceratopians.

This small animal had some original ornithopod characteristics such as a chiefly bipedal stance and long fingers. It did not yet possess the bony neck frill, a trademark of many ceratopians, but already it showed another of their trademarks: the parrot-like beak and grinding cheek-teeth. The appearance of this type of jaw, not seen before among dinosaurs, approximately corresponds with the appearance of flowering plants (angiosperms) during the Cretaceous period. It could have been an adaptation which allowed these animals to eat these new types of plants, while most herbivorous dinosaurs still fed off the gymnosperms – but as yet, there is no strong evidence to suggest this is true.

SALTASAURUS

Classification Order Saurischia, Suborder Sauropodomorpha
Age Late Cretaceous, 70 million years ago
Measurements Height 16 ft, length 39 ft
Fossil sites South America
Notes This animal is named for the place where it was first discovered, Salta. Although it was largely a typical sauropod, it is unusual in that its skin was covered in body nodules and plates, probably as armored protection against predators. It had a powerful tail and, like many other members of its group, it could support itself by tail and back legs as it reared up to snatch the leaves from the tops of trees.

  16 39

SAUROLOPHUS

Classification Order Ornithischia, Suborder Ornithopoda
Age Late Cretaceous, 70 million years ago
Measurements Height 14 ft, length 30–40 ft
Fossil sites North America, Asia
Notes *Saurolophus* means "ridged reptile," referring to the ridge of bone on the front of the face, which ended in a small spike at the top of the skull. Many hadrosaurs had these ridges or crests on their heads, which were probably used for social communication.

  14 30–40

SCELIDOSAURUS

Classification Order Ornithischia, Suborder Thyreophora
Age Jurassic, 190 million years ago
Measurements Height about 4 ft, length 13 ft, heavily built
Fossil sites England, USA, Tibet
Notes *Scelidosaurus* means "limb reptile." This small animal was an early armored dinosaur. Its relationships are uncertain but it may have been an early cousin of the Stegosaurs.

STEGOSAURUS

Classification Order Ornithischia, Suborder Stegosauria
Age Late Jurassic, 150 million years ago
Measurements Height 12 ft, length 12–27 ft
Fossil sites North America
Notes *Stegosaurus* means "roofed reptile." Although there are many good specimens of this animal, nobody is still absolutely sure how the back plates were arranged or what their function was. They were probably in two upright rows, staggered slightly, and were most likely used for temperature regulation. The animal would stand side-on to the sun when it needed to warm itself, and end-on in a breeze or in the shade when it was too hot. It used the spines on its tail for defense.

12

12–27

STRUTHIOMIMUS

Classification Order Saurischia, Suborder Therapoda
Age Late Cretaceous, 75 million years ago
Measurements Height 7 ft, length 10–13 ft
Fossil sites North America
Notes *Struthiomimus*, the "ostrich mimic," had skeletal proportions very similar to those of a modern ostrich.

Scientists believe they lived in much the same way. This able-bodied runner could obviously travel fast, preying on and snapping up anything it could find.

TARBOSAURUS

Classification Order Saurischia, Suborder Theropoda
Age Late Cretaceous, 70 million years ago
Measurements Height about 16 ft, length 35 ft
Fossil sites Mongolia, China
Notes *Tarbosaurus* means, appropriately, "alarming reptile." Although it comes from the other side of the world to *Tyrannosaurus*, there are many close similarities. Minor differences are in the skull, and in adults which did not reach the great size of *Tyrannosaurus*, but these two types of dinosaur were almost certainly closely related and probably lived similar lifestyles.

TENONTOSAURUS

Classification Order Ornithischia, Suborder Ornithopoda
Age Cretaceous, 110 million years ago
Measurements Height about 7 ft, length 24 ft, weight 1 ton
Fossil sites North America
Notes *Tenontosaurus* means "sinew reptile." It was one of the largest members of its group. The very long and powerful tail may have been used in defense against predatory dinosaurs. It probably moved more on its back legs, especially when

traveling at speed, with the extremely long tail held out straight behind. Its head was proportionally larger than the ornithopod design, it had a bony beak at the front of its mouth, and it had more complicated teeth which were capable of initially breaking down food before it was swallowed.

TOROSAURUS

Classification Order Ornithischia, Suborder Ceratopia
Age Late Cretaceous, 70 million years ago
Measurements Height 12 ft, length 25 ft
Fossil sites North America
Notes *Torosaurus*, the "bull reptile," is only known from remains of its head, which had the largest neck frill of all ceratopians and one of the largest skulls of any known land animal. The frill and the skull both measured 8½ ft. One specimen of *Torosaurus* shows signs of what is thought to be bone cancer.

TRICERATOPS

Classification Order Ornithischia, Suborder Ceratopia
Age Late Cretaceous, 66 million years ago
Measurements Height 10 ft, length 30 ft, weight 5–6 tons
Fossil sites North America
Notes The well-known *Triceratops*, or "three-horned face," was one of the last surviving dinosaurs. The two eyebrow horns on its face may have been well over 3 ft long in life, while the skull from the nose to the end of the neck frill measured 11½ ft. The animal was large and heavy but *Triceratops* could probably have moved at speed for short distances; when provoked it would charge, bringing the nose horn up to slash the underbelly of any predator standing over it. The solid frill would prevent the teeth of the carnivore grabbing lumps of flesh.

  10 30

BELOW *Young* Triceratops *compared to rhinoceros; an adult would be about twice the size of a modern rhino.*

TYRANNOSAURUS

Classification Order Saurischia, Suborder Theropoda
Age Late Cretaceous, 70 million years ago
Measurements Height 20 ft, length 40 ft, weight 7 tons
Fossil sites North America
Notes Famed as one of the largest known land-dwelling flesh-eaters that has ever lived, its name means "tyrant reptile." Its likely food sources were plant-eating dinosaurs such as hadrosaurs, and scavenged carrion. Its head was 4 ft long and the jaws contained serrated teeth 6 in long. They may have used their tiny front legs to help swing the huge head into the air when getting up from the ground.

Tyrannosaurus

ULTRASAURUS

Classification Order Saurischia, Suborder Sauropodomorpha
Possible Measurements Length 98 ft, weight 100 tons
Fossil sites Colorado, USA
Notes *Ultrasaurus* means "ultra reptile" and it is believed to be around the limits of size for a land vertebrate. It is only known from a few leg bones, but it could have been one-third larger than *Brachiosaurus*. It has not yet been fully scientifically described or named. Another recent fossil find, dubbed *"Seismosaurus,"* could have been as big or even bigger.

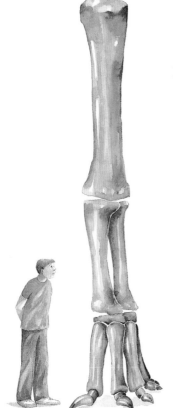

The leg bones of Ultrasaurus *compared to* Brachiosaurus *and to the size of humans.*

INDEX

Page numbers in *italics* refer to picture captions.

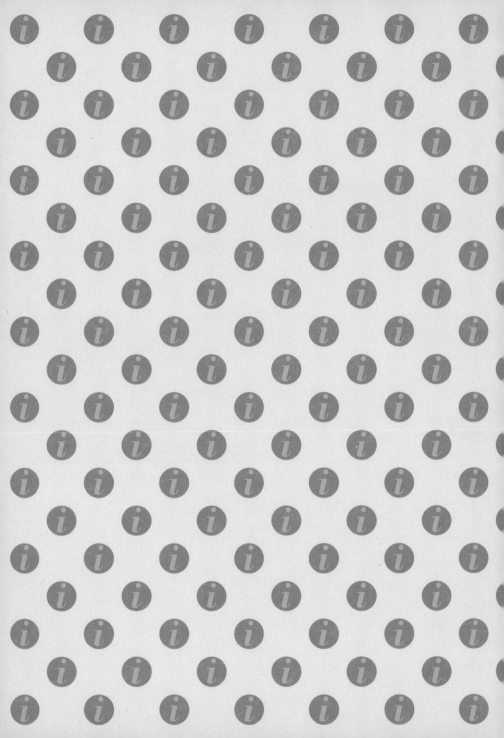